# DRAWINGS
# HOLBEIN

# DRAWINGS
# HOLBEIN

## by
## František Dvořák

**3M Books**
**St. Paul, Minnesota**
**1985**

HANS HOLBEIN THE YOUNGER: Drawings

by František Dvořák

Designer: Aleš Krejča

Supervising editor, English language edition: Pamela Espeland
Translated from the German by Christa Tiefenbacher-Hudson
Designers, English language edition: Evans-Smith & Skubic, Incorporated

Library of Congress Cataloging in Publication Data

Holbein, Hans, 1497-1543.
  Holbein: drawings.

  Translation of: Hans Holbein mladší
  Bibliography: p.
  1. Holbein, Hans, 1497-1543. 2. Artists—Germany—Biography.
  I. Dvořák, František. II. Title.
NC251.H65D8513  1985          741.943                    84-23939
ISBN 0-88159-803-8

Distributed to the trade by the Putnam Publishing Group
Printed in Czechoslovakia

# CONTENTS

# Notes on the Collotype Process

To achieve the most accurate reproductions possible of Hans Holbein the Younger's drawings, the publishers of this volume have elected to use a special photographic process called *collotype*. This expensive and old-fashioned printing method was invented in 1855 and put into commercial use in 1868. At most, it can produce only a few thousand copies, yet because of its ability to render fine detail it remains in demand for short runs of fine art prints of illustrations and for limited editions of books.

A collotype is made on a sheet of ground glass coated with bichromated gelatin. The plate is first dried in an oven until the gelatin reticulates into a pattern of almost microscopic cracks. A continuous-tone negative is then held up to the plate and light is passed through both the plate and the negative, causing the gelatin to harden in direct proportion to the tones of the negative.

Following this step the plate is washed to remove the bichromate and treated with a glycerine solution that moistens the areas which remained less hard after their exposure to light. A greasy lithographic ink is then rolled over the plate. The ink is repelled by the moist areas but accepted by the tiny reticulation cracks of the dry, hardened areas. Finally, paper is pressed against the plate and the image is transferred.

The collotype process is unsuitable for long print runs due to the fact that the delicate gelatin surface begins to slowly deteriorate after approximately one thousand copies are made. Without the gelatin, however, it would not be possible to reproduce with such accuracy the detailing and shading of the original work of art. Thus, while the process does not lend itself to mass production, it does result in superb prints that capture the beauty and intensity of Hans Holbein the Younger's drawings.

For this volume the collotype process was used to reproduce each of the 35 black-and-white plates. The 22 color plates, and the art within the text, were reproduced by the more usual method of offset printing.

# IN THE COURT
# OF KING HENRY VIII

*If someone should unmask the actors in the middle of a scene on the stage and show their real faces to the audience, would he not spoil the whole play?*
　　　　　　　　—Erasmus, *In Praise of Folly*

Nearly a century before Shakespeare penned the lines, "All the world's a stage, and men and women merely players," the humanist philosopher Desiderius Erasmus wrote, "Now what else is our whole life but a kind of stage play through which men pass in various disguises, each one going on to play his part until he is led off by the director? ...Thus everything is pretense; yet this play is performed in no other way."

The court of King Henry VIII in the time of Erasmus — and Hans Holbein the Younger — was the stage for one of the most passion-filled dramas in history, and it rivaled any Italian Renaissance court in brilliance. While Holbein did not "unmask" any of the players with his delicate brush, he was an astute observer of the scene as well as an unobtrusive actor in the drama itself.

Holbein first traveled to England in 1526; he was not yet thirty years old. He was already an artist of some repute, having practiced his craft in Basel, Switzerland for nine years. He brought with him the tools of his trade and a few letters of introduction from Erasmus, who had encouraged him to go "scrape some angels together." The letters gave Holbein a privileged entrée to the court of King Henry VIII through Erasmus's friends Sir Thomas More, then undersecretary of the treasury and soon to become Lord Chancellor, and Lord Montjoy, a cousin of Bessie Blount, who would later bear Henry an illegitimate son.

We don't know what Holbein expected when he arrived in England, but we do know what he found: a dazzling spectacle. The youthful King Henry had inherited the gloomy court left by his father, Henry VII, and transformed it. Gone were the dark plotting and intrigue, replaced by a style of life

1

that Catherine of Aragon described as "a continuous festival." Henry VII's penny-pinching ways had filled the treasury and his son used it to create a new magnificence, making the court a center of cultural and social life unlike anything England had ever known.

In contrast to his dour old forebear, Henry VIII was, in his people's eyes, an ideal kingly figure. Nearly six feet tall, he had a commanding presence and towered over most of his companions — and many other monarchs. Before an ulcerated leg curtailed exercise, he was exceptionally well-proportioned and athletic. Clean-shaven and fair-complected, he had short, straight auburn hair and a slightly rounded face with delicately formed features that some said "would have been called pretty in a woman."

His *joie de vivre* was infectious. He loved "entertainments" of all kinds, taking the lead in tournaments and jousts, commanding the tennis courts and outlasting his horses in the hunt. He could dance half the night and drink most men under the table, and he derived great pleasure from dressing up for pageants and masks, which he introduced from Italy. An account of a Twelfth Night celebration dating from that time describes what it was like when the King and eleven of his courtiers attended the banquet:

> [They came in] disguised after the manner of Italy, called a mask, a thing not seen afore in England. They were apparelled in garments long and broad, wrought all with gold, with vizers and caps of gold; and after the banquet was done, the maskers came in with six gentlemen disguised in silk, bearing staff torches, and desired the ladies to dance....And after they danced and communed together, as the fashion of the mask is, they took their leave and departed, and so did the Queen and all her ladies.

Henry enjoyed masquerading so much that he once "invaded" Queen Catherine's chambers with a dozen men dressed in the "Kentish" fashion — in other words, like Robin Hood's band — and only revealed themselves after dancing with all the ladies. Many years later Henry tried the same prank with Anne of Cleves before their wedding; Anne was not amused.

Henry was also exceedingly fond of music and enticed the finest musicians from England and the continent to his court. His organist was the acclaimed Venetian Friar Denis Memmo, who left his post at St. Mark's in Venice and brought his own instrument with him. English musicians played the stringed instruments; the brass and woodwind players hailed from Flanders, Milan, Cremona and Germany.

Along with the musicians came artists and scholars. The artists included Pietro Torrigiano, who had been working for the Borgias in Rome and was known for his violent temper; he had the dubious distinction of having dealt the blow which permanently disfigured Michelangelo's nose. Also present were Antonio Toto, who had studied under Ghirlandaio; John Corvus of Bruges; Lucas Horenbout of Ghent; and, of course, Hans Holbein the Younger of Augsburg, who was to outshine them all.

The court of Henry VIII had what we would call "high visibility" today. The city of London itself was still a walled, medieval enclave, covering one square mile, but within it and the surrounding "home counties" Henry had many palaces and he ranged among them often. There were Westminster and the White Tower, Windsor, Brideswell, Baynard's Castle, Richmond, Greenwich, Eltham, Woodstock, and later Whitehall and Hampton Court, acquired from Cardinal Wolsey. When the King moved, the court moved with him and the streets were filled with pageants, processions, music and laughter.

Chelsea was a district south of London bordering the Thames, and it was there that Holbein was welcomed into the household of Sir Thomas More. Though More lived modestly, abstaining from wine and rich foods, his home must have been quite lively. He entertained scholars, philosophers, astronomers and the famous lyric poet, Thomas Wyatt, among others. More had an open face, with a clear complexion and blue-gray eyes, and was noted for his sense of humor as well as his intellect. His contemporary Robert Whittington described him as "a man of an angel's wit, and singular learning....And as time requireth, a man of marvellous mirth and pastimes, and sometimes of as sad gravity...A man for all seasons." Erasmus characterized More's household as one "where you would realize that Plato's academy was revived." The King himself was known to drop in on More unexpectedly and walk with him in the garden, his royal arm draped across the older man's shoulders.

Among Holbein's first commissions were a portrait of Thomas More and a group painting of More with his family. (When Holbein left England after two years, in 1528, he took the latter with him as a gift for Erasmus.) During this period he also completed portraits of the astronomer Nicklaus Kratzer, Sir Nicholas Carew, Bishop John Fisher, Sir Henry Wyatt, Sir Henry Guildford and William Warham, Archbishop of Canterbury.

Though Holbein was not yet "officially" at court, a commission in 1527 to work on the construction of a temporary banquet hall at Greenwich gave him a taste of Henry's sumptuous entertainments and extravagant style. The occasion was an agreement with Francis I of France that Henry and Catherine's daughter Mary would be betrothed to Francis or one of his sons in the future (an agreement which was never realized). The banquet hall was 100 feet long and 30 feet wide, arched at each end by antique burnished pillars decorated with gargoyles and serpents. The roof was covered with a purple cloth adorned with roses and pomegranates. There were windows, a stage for minstrels, and cupboards for gold and silver plates. Accounts show that Holbein was paid more than the other workers on the project, indicating that his skills were already highly valued.

It seemed to many like a golden age, but it was already drawing to a close. Three years before Holbein's arrival the King had become infatuated with one of the Queen's ladies. Although she was discharged from service and sent back to her home in Hever, Henry's passion remained unabated. He made frequent unannounced visits to Hever. By 1527 the snake was in the garden — and Anne Boleyn was back in court. Whispers and rumors of witchcraft were heard. Anne had a rudimentary sixth finger on her left hand, and a "devil's paw-mark" — a mole — on her throat. The Holy Nun of Kent, Elizabeth Barton, predicted that if Henry divorced Catherine England would suffer dire calamities.

Holbein left London and returned to his family in Basel in 1528. If the luxurious style of Henry's court had not suited his classical tastes, the excesses of Protestant Reformers must have pleased him even less. He was a Protestant himself but a follower of Erasmus, and like his teacher he hoped for a rational resolution of differences. It was not to be. The Basel Reformers sacked the churches, destroying centuries of priceless "idolatrous" art.

Without the patronage of the church, there was little work for artists. Holbein bought a house, perhaps intending to wait things out, but the lack of commissions and the rising tide of destruction around him drove him back to England after only four years.

He must have seen in people's faces how drastically things had changed. The year 1532 was not a happy one for London. Queen Catherine had been asked to move from Windsor to a residence called The More, and Anne was ensconced at Whitehall (where one day Holbein would have his studio). All of this was unsettling and the subject of much gossip, but even more disturbing was the fact that Henry was risking a schism with the Catholic Church in Rome. If Henry was excommunicated, which was a distinct possibility given his behavior, then all allegiances sworn to him would be considered nullified — and England would be divided and ripe for invasion.

More and his friends were out of favor, not yet imprisoned in the Tower but exiled from the court. In just three years More's head and Fisher's would be hoisted on pikes set out on London Bridge.

With his former patrons in distressing and dangerous circumstances, caught up in the King's battle with the Church, Holbein, either by calculation or natural inclination, gravitated to a circle of successful German merchants who formed the Hanseatic League. During this period he did many of their portraits. They are usually shown dressed in sober black and looking rather serious-minded. They are pictured in their rooms or offices, which are simple and unadorned except for various practical objects relating to each man's enterprise. The Hanseatic League was a powerful political group largely because of its ties to Maximilian II, archduke of Austria and king of Hungary and Bohemia who would be crowned Holy Roman Emperor in 1564.

Though the general atmosphere of London was subdued, Henry's gala festivities went on unabated. Anne accompanied him everywhere despite the silent crowds who showed little enthusiasm for Henry's new Queen-in-waiting. Henry evidenced his own favor ostentatiously. Breaking all precedents, he made Anne the Marquis of Pembroke — a rank no woman in England had ever before held in her own right. Holbein may well have been present at the grand ceremony; he almost certainly attended Anne's coronation a few months later, for he designed one of the pageant arches.

The ceremony went on for three whole days in May of 1533. There was a great water carnival, and Anne was rowed to the Tower in a barge bedecked with bunting, ribbons and wreaths of flowers. Hundreds of smaller craft escorted her. Her dress was of gold cloth and her long, black hair hung below her waist. The Tower had been refurbished, gilded and glazed and festooned with new hangings. On the third day Anne was carried by litter through the streets to Westminster to be crowned.

Henry and Anne were already secretly married. In January the King had learned that she was pregnant and had wed her almost immediately in a small, private ceremony either at Whitehall or Greenwich. He was determined that his heir would be legitimate; either the Pope would annul his former marriage to Catherine or he would repudiate the Pope's authority.

It was probably around this time that Holbein reestablished his connections with the court. He painted the King's falconer that year and also completed one of his finest paintings, *The Ambassadors*, of the two men who carried messages to and from the Pope.

The decision came at last: the Pope proclaimed that Henry would have to give up Anne and take Catherine back as his lawful wife. Henry was given one more chance when Pope Clement died before the date he had set for the King's compliance; the new Pope, Paul III, was soon hearing Henry's petitions. He, however, upheld Clement's ruling. Henry responded with his Act of Succession (ensuring his heir, Elizabeth, who had been born in July, her right to the throne) and then his Act of Supremacy. The latter declared Henry to be Head of the Church, something neither More nor Fisher could swear to uphold. The two of them were beheaded in 1535.

The King also launched a brutal attack on the Carthusians, a sect who opposed the Act of Supremacy, and had its members tortured and eviscerated. None of them recanted. More's final words were said to be, "I die the King's good servant — but God's first." When he was brought word of More's death, Henry is reported to have turned to Anne and shouted, "It is because of you the honestest man in my kingdom is dead!"

Apparently Henry's affection for Anne Boleyn subsided soon

after the wedding. Perhaps nine years of waiting had built up expectations that were bound to be disappointed. The birth of a girl child, Elizabeth, instead of the boy Henry wanted was followed in the next few years by three miscarriages.

These events gave Henry pause for thought — and what he thought was that he should take another wife.

He assigned Thomas Cromwell, Earl of Essex, the task of getting rid of Anne. Cromwell did so with his usual cunning and efficiency. Placing spies around the palace and possibly employing physical intimidation on Mark Smeaton, a young musician who sometimes played for Anne, he procured the evidence he wanted. Smeaton confessed to adultery with the Queen and named five other men as well. (Thomas Wyatt was among them, but he was later released from prison and brought back into the King's favor.) Cromwell took the legal position that adultery in a Queen was treason — and treason was a capital offense.

At first Henry pretended to be surprised and shocked, but then he pronounced that he was ready to believe that Anne had slept with a hundred men. Meanwhile his courtship of Jane Seymour was well underway. The day after Anne was accused, the King was rowed upriver to dine with Jane. Chapuys, the Spanish ambassador, wrote, "You never saw prince or other man who displayed his horns more or wore them more gladly."

In May of 1536 the court convened and found Anne and her alleged suitors guilty. A special swordsman from Calais was imported to serve as executioner. The day after Anne's beheading, Henry married Jane Seymour in the Queen's Chapel at Whitehall.

During the brief interlude of quiet and seeming happiness when Jane was pregnant and Henry content, Holbein was commissioned to paint a fresco on the walls of the Privy Chamber showing Queen Jane, the King, and his parents, of the Houses of York and Lancaster, awaiting the royal birth. Though known today only through copies, this painting seems to have been the prototype of Holbein's famous full portrait of Henry VIII. Henry dominates the picture, massive, jaunty, with his legs apart and his feet firmly on the ground — an image of supreme power. This image, which Holbein was to paint several times, has determined posterity's conception of England's oft-wed king.

Cromwell is said to have been responsible for singling out Holbein as the artist who would present the face of the new monarchy to the world. Holbein's Protestantism, as well as his talent, may have been a deciding factor. Holbein was commissioned to create a title page for Coverdale's new translation of the Bible. He portrayed Henry sitting on the throne, holding the sword of justice in his right hand and giving the Book to his kneeling bishops with his left. The picture gave visual dramatization to the words of Coverdale's dedication: "He only under God is the Chief Head of all the congregation and the church."

Holbein painted Jane Seymour, Cromwell and later Edward, the young Prince of Wales. Though busy with portraits of royalty and other members of the court, Holbein never lost his humanist point of view and also continued

painting people of the middle and lower classes. He painted one of the maids at Whitehall and Mistress Jak, Prince Edward's wet nurse.

Twelve days after the birth of the prince, Jane Seymour died — and the King started looking for yet another wife. It was in this part of the ongoing drama that Holbein played his most active role.

Cromwell had convinced Henry of the advantage of a foreign match coupled with an alliance to end England's isolation. There were ample prospects to choose from: the Continent was bursting with princesses. Henry was first taken with the idea of marrying a young widow of 16, Christina, Duchess of Milan, the daughter of Christian II of Denmark and niece of Emperor Charles V. He sent Holbein to Brussels to paint her. When the King saw the painting, he was delighted and decided to have her. The conditions he outlined, however, and the complication of her being related to his first wife Catherine (the Emperor insisted on a Papal dispensation) resulted in the breakdown of negotiations.

Henry next turned his gaze toward France, where five princesses were waiting. He suggested to Francis I that they all be brought to Calais for a sort of beauty pageant, with the Queen along to act as chaperon. Francis was shocked and replied that the knights of the Round Table had been more chivalrous. Henry insisted, "The thing touches me too near. I wish to see them...." Since he couldn't spend his time traveling the Continent to find the one who would suit his tastes, he again dispatched Holbein with instructions to paint each one of them in turn.

Holbein went first to Havre to paint the Duchess Louise of Guise, then to Nancy and Joinville where he saw Anne of Lorraine and Renée of Guise. Meanwhile Charles V and Francis met and signed a treaty. It outlined the terms of peace between them and their agreement to suppress the Protestant heresies. Almost simultaneously the long-awaited Papal bull came, deposing Henry and absolving his subjects from their allegiance to him.

For the next three years England lived under the threat of invasion and Henry built up his defenses. In seeking allies, he turned in desperation to the German princes. He needed a German bride. The Duke of Cleves had two marriageable sisters, Anne and Amelia. Though both had already been painted by Lucas Cranach, Henry claimed that he couldn't see them well enough because of the "monstrous habits" they wore for their portraits. Holbein was sent off once more. When Henry inspected the portraits, he settled on Anne.

The arrangements were made and the King waited impatiently for the woman who would be his fourth wife. A few days before her scheduled arrival in London, Henry rode on horseback with five members of his Privy Chamber, all disguised in hoods and cloaks, to her quarters in Rochester. Pretending to have come from the King bearing a gift, he tried to embrace her. Even when he revealed who he was, she was so disturbed that she couldn't speak — at least not in English, which, Henry discovered with dismay, she didn't know.

He was profoundly disappointed. Anne was rather dull and unaccomplished and Henry did not find her physically attractive. As if that weren't enough, the two of them literally could not talk to one another. The marriage took place but was never consummated. Within a fairly short time Henry's interest was sparked by one of Anne's maids of honor, Catherine Howard. There was no problem having this marriage annulled. Working through a translator, Henry learned that Anne was quite agreeable to changing her situation. Dubbing her his "adopted sister," he set her up in a household of her own with a generous yearly stipend.

Holbein witnessed the brief, tragic drama of Catherine Howard's rise and fall, which must have reminded him of the days of Anne Boleyn. Within two years of the wedding, Catherine was accused of adultery. She was tried and executed in February of 1542. Holbein himself died the following year of the plague.


Art historians have commented about the singular expressions on the faces of Hans Holbein the Younger's subjects. There is a similarity among them, and while the paintings fully reveal physical reality in distinctive features the personalities are hidden.

Although we will never know precisely why Holbein chose to paint in this manner, a number of possible explanations have been suggested. One simple and practical reason may have been that posing for long periods of time does not lend itself to a variety of expressions but instead to a few that are comfortable. Another may be traced back to Holbein's humanist beliefs, which may well have prompted him to seek the "essential" person (in the spirit of Plato's idealized forms) behind the individual. Still another possibility might rest in the fact that at Henry VIII's court, showing one's true face often meant losing one's head. We cannot fault Holbein for allowing the players he portrayed to wear their masks. As Erasmus noted, doing otherwise would have spoiled the play.

# THE DRAWINGS OF HANS HOLBEIN THE YOUNGER

*He fulfills his life completely in his art; no element of his personality survives in his work.*
    —Hans Reinhardt, *Holbein*

One might assume that a book published today on the drawings of Hans Holbein the Younger would have little to say that has not been said before. In the more than four centuries following his death, countless art historians and scholars have studied his works. The topic should be exhausted; our conception of the artist should be fixed.

But the laws of human progress demand that we continually reexamine our relationship to the classics. A painting, a drawing, a poem, a piece of music — each brings with it a legacy that must be viewed from the perspective of our own experience. Classics are classics because they still speak to us, still move us. If we are lucky — or, more to the point, open and perceptive — we sometimes discover meanings that have lain dormant.

Holbein's art is rooted in the past, but it is not confined to it. Although the faces of his subjects mirror the epoch that shaped his work, they are as fresh and immediate today as they were when the artist put down his chalk. Their appeal and their power have endured for these hundreds of years. We study them not because they are old but because they remain so new. We can, and should, read what others who came before us have had to say about them; it is only when we see them for ourselves, however, that we realize how much is left to learn.

Following the practice common among painters of the past, Hans Holbein the Younger appears to have made most of his drawings as preparations for paintings. He incorporated some of them into final compositions with no changes. Yet even the most preliminary studies seem independent and complete in themselves; each reveals the artist's personality and mastery of style.

When we judge drawings on their own merits — in other words, as separate from the paintings they preceded — we are adopting a critical stance of fairly recent origins. It was not until the beginning of the nineteenth century that drawing was accorded more than second-class status in terms of its perceived artistic value. While nobody today insists that the drawings of Picasso or Klee be linked to other "final" works, it was still somewhat revolutionary for the contemporaries of Daumier and Cézanne and Toulouse-Lautrec to view their drawings as capable of standing alone. Knowing this helps us to appreciate how very unusual it was for an artist in the early sixteenth century to place drawing on a level equal to that of painting, as Holbein did.

Hans Holbein the Younger was born in Augsburg, Germany, second only to Nuremberg at the time as Germany's richest city. Although the precise date of his birth is not known, it is generally assumed to have been in late 1497 or early 1498. Augsburg was located on an old trade route which had grown in importance with the opening of new sea routes and the transportation of valuable merchandise to and across Europe. In 1505 Augsburg merchants like the Fugger, Welser, Hochstätter and Gosenbrot families participated in a Portuguese expedition to the East Indies. The wealthiest among them, the Fugger family, also managed to win the exclusive right to mine copper in Slovakia (Czechoslovakia) and exported it in such large quantities that no other European concern could compete. Later they opened silver mines in Slovakia and Turkey, eventually emerging as the most powerful mining entrepreneurs in all of Europe. In addition to running the mining business, Jakob II (1459-1525), called "Jakob the Rich," traded in spices, served as papal banker, made loans to Maximilian I (1459-1519) and financed the election of Charles V (1500-1558).

These early European capitalists did not seem particularly involved or interested in either the arts or the sciences. No apparent connection can be found, for example, between their wealth and sixteenth-century Augsburg's cultural scene. Unlike the moneyed houses of the Italian Renaissance, they owned neither libraries nor art collections. Their names are associated with a single artistic venture: the family chapel in the church of Saint Anna. Its sculptural decorations were executed by Adolf Daucher according to drafts drawn by Albrecht Dürer (1471-1528). Completed in 1518, they are believed to represent the first Renaissance work of art in Germany and were probably commissioned by some patron following the example set by Pope Julius II (1443-1513).

Hans Holbein the Elder (1465?-1524), himself a painter, had no business dealings with the Fugger clan, but ten portraits of family members have been preserved in his sketchbook, including one of Jakob the Rich. It is not known whether these were commissioned or stemmed from a personal interest on the part of the artist; no paintings survive that can be traced back to them.

Hans Holbein the Younger spent his apprentice years in his father's studio, reputed to be Augsburg's premiere school of painting. Even in his youth the son seemed to take stylistic liberties which the father, dependent on commissions for his living, could ill afford. The difference between the elder's private studies and his commissioned works is worth noting. It is evident, for example, in the double portrait of Hans the Younger and his brother, Ambrosius, drawn in 1511 *(see page 9)*. Here the father has turned away from the stylized structure that otherwise bound his hand. The figures curve naturally, their hair looks soft, and their clothing clings to their bodies as real fabric would rather than hanging in stiff, artificial folds. When we compare this work to other portraits from the same period, we see remarkable dissimilarities. Consider, for instance, virtually any drawing by Dürer, Holbein the Elder's most eminent contemporary. Dürer was able to render a portrait with astonishing accuracy, but the direction of his line is obviously fixed and thought out in advance; his shading, accomplished with parallel strokes, is graphically stylized; and the fall of the clothing deforms reality in keeping with the late Gothic mode.

According to Alfred Woltmann, one of his biographers, Hans Holbein the Elder left Augsburg in 1517 and moved to Isenheim, both because of his debts and because he felt overshadowed by other artists including Hans Burgkmair (1473-1531) and Breu. Today, however, we know that Maximilian I held him in especially high esteem and, by a special decree, released him from having to observe the regulations of the artists' guild. Nor, it seems, were his debts a deciding factor; he owed the largest to his brother Sigmund. Perhaps he felt that he would find elsewhere the recognition he sought.[1]

T he double portrait mentioned above is the first known portrayal of Hans Holbein the Younger. On it the number 14 is written above the boy's head, indicating his age at the time. The Holbeins were a family of artists: a grandfather was a goldsmith; the elder and his brother Sigmund were both painters and worked together; the younger Hans showed definite talent, and his brother Ambrosius also took up the brush. Little else is known about our subject's youth.

From the style of his father's drawings, we may assume that all of the Holbeins were familiar with the leading Italian artists of that era. Holbein the Elder may even have visited the Netherlands; one of his drawings, now in Basel, indicates that he had a thorough knowledge of the works of Hugo van der Goes (1440?-1482). Others reveal the influence of Leonardo da Vinci (1452-1519).

To round out his sons' education, Holbein the Elder sent both of them to Switzerland. Ambrosius, three years older than Hans, was the first to go. He traveled to Lake Constance in 1514, spent some time there, and probably visited Stein on the Rhine as well before moving on to Basel; a document from the year 1517 proves that he became a Master Artist there. Two years later he fled the city because of the plague. Several very delicately done drawings and a series of woodcuts whose ornamentation indicates an excellent creative imagination attest to the relationship between Ambrosius's art and his father's studio. Ambrosius died in either 1519 or 1520 at the age of twenty-five.

Hans Holbein the Younger's journey led him directly to Basel, where he arrived in 1515. It is likely that he was attracted to the enlightened humanists who made that city their home. Beatus Rhenanus (1485-1547) and Bonifacius Amerbach (1496?-1562) gave him a traditional classical education.[2] Hans also made the acquaintance of the well-known printer Johann Froben (1460?-1527), who was busy publishing the works of contemporary humanists. The person who influenced him the most, however, was probably Desiderius Erasmus (1466?-1536) of Rotterdam, originally Gerhard Gerhards, called simply Erasmus and the most famous man of his time. A Dutch scholar whose Greek New Testament was published by Froben in 1516, Erasmus was credited with leading the renaissance of learning in northern Europe.

An essay on the cooperation between these two personalities reveals Erasmus's affect on Holbein's early works and the ideas the artist drew from him for his later creative efforts.[3] Holbein and Erasmus searched together for the stoical, enlightened ideal of the man of deeds guided by humanism — the classical ideal of the free personality whose freedom is tempered by truth, education and beauty. Both men believed that humankind's state could be elevated were a strong ruler educated by humanists to come to power. They saw the realization of their dream in the reign of the English King Henry VIII (1491-1547), and both later went to his court.

Erasmus had a profound knowledge of the Greek and Roman classics, and these in turn inspired him to pursue an understanding of general human traits. He expressed his principles in his moralistic work *Ritter vom Thurn* (The Knight from Thurn) and in *Encomium moriae* (In Praise of Folly). Holbein incorporated these principles into his art; his perception of reality as expressed by artistic means was founded on them.

Holbein disapproved of the prevailing styles of his time; none of his Middle European contemporaries distanced themselves as thoroughly as he did from the late Gothic and old German modes. He preferred instead the pure forms of ancient Greece. His works are idealized, objectified, devoid of elements which might help us to place their subjects within specific physical or temporal settings. He depicted living, breathing men and women, yet somehow they are something more: each, whether king or philosopher, clergyman or courtier, glows with the classical, timeless ideal of beauty.

Holbein dwelt exclusively on the human face and body and showed almost no interest in the landscapes that were so popular during the development of Renaissance painting.[4] (See, for example, the works of the German painters Albrecht Altdorfer [1480?-1538], Lucas Cranach [1472-1553], and Wolf Huber, and the Swiss painters Urs Graf, Hans Leu and Nikolaus Manuel [1484-1530].) Neither did he follow in the footsteps of Dürer, who by the end of the fifteenth century was one generation older than Holbein and had already completed a series of watercolors on nature themes.

Holbein sought to capture the "permanent" face — not the one that reveals passing feelings or moods. Thus his portraits are almost expressionless. The problems of illustrating age, character traits and individual qualities took second place to his goal of creating art which was purely conceptual in the Platonic sense of the word. Occasionally he added extraneous details to his pictures — perhaps a portion of an interior — and these details sometimes became independent studies, but he never incorporated immediately observed nature. The only known exceptions are the landscapes that occasionally served as a frame for a religious scene.[5] To him, the only world worth painting was that of the human phenomenon.

It is likely that this outlook was a direct result of his studies among the humanists in Basel. Through artistic means, he approached the question of how human limitations could be overcome; to arrive at an answer, he sought the stimulation of intellectual and artistic companions. We may assume that he found them among the group of erudite personalities associated with Froben's printing and publishing house. Erasmus was the editor there; working closely with him was Beatus Rhenanus, who had arrived in Basel in 1511 with the Bohemian humanist Zikmund Hrubý, called Gelenius. Other leading figures of the time were Ludwig Bär, dean of the theological faculty at the university; Wolfgang Fabricius Capito, a German clergyman and supporter of Martin Luther; the theologian Ökolampadius; and the painter Urs Graf.

B asel had been an excellent place to get a good classical education since 1501, when the city had succeeded in freeing itself from its obligations toward the German Empire and become a member of the Swiss Confederation. Politically, this had made Basel an ally of Venice and the pope, which in turn had opened the way to the south almost overnight. In 1515 the Swiss were defeated by the French King Francis I (1494-1547), whose invasion of Italy had previously changed the nature of the relationships between Europe's rulers. Once such foreign affairs were formally settled, Basel relinquished its former expansionist policy and established a democratic patrician system in keeping with the growing economic power of the middle class.

Within the city government, increasing pressures were felt to administer a moral and harmonious lifestyle. Philosophical-ethical humanism seemed suited both to this emphasis and to the city's historical situation. Holbein, coming out of a feudal environment, looked upon the emergence of the middle class and recognized the opportunity it presented. His talents were suited to the developing ideology. Humanism awarded humankind the central position in society, an attitude of which Holbein approved and deemed more important than privilege or the protection of a powerful ruler. While Leonardo sought the favor of such eminences as Francesco Sforza of Milan and, later, Cesare Borgia and the King of France, Holbein viewed the artist's calling to produce beautiful works as a democratic function.

John Ruskin once observed that the best pictures of the painters from the great schools are portraits. The cultural milieu of sixteenth-century Basel was remarkable not only because it gave the world living translations of classical literature and philosophy and freed humankind from its medieval bonds, but also because it produced the finest portraitist north of the Alps. The humanists with whom Holbein surrounded himself were a new breed; they perceived the human soul with new eyes. If his renderings of human faces and scenes from everyday life evidenced a certain idealism, so did his social circle. His preference for the portrait was in keeping with the aphorism of Socrates that was widely quoted at the time: "It is not the trees but the people I am interested in."

Although Holbein was not yet twenty when he arrived in Basel, he already had some experience and learning behind him. We may presume that he knew Leonardo's book, *Trattato della Pittura* (Treatise on Painting). In it da Vinci outlined a number of important concepts: that the painter should be the mediator between reality and art; that a portrait had to reveal the sureness of the creative instinct; and that artists were expected to master their craft by constantly practicing it. It is equally probable that Holbein had read a study of the paintings of Leon Battista Alberti (1404-1472) written in 1435, which mentions numerous creative principles which he subsequently brought to bear in his own efforts, including the function of the drawing when modeling forms and the importance of thoroughly familiarizing oneself with the human form. Finally, there is little doubt that he had acquired a store of technical knowledge from the *Trattato della Pittura* of Cennino Cennini (*c.* 1370-*c.* 1440); according to Vasari, it was quite popular in those days. As we read Cennini today, we can almost envision Hans Holbein the Younger preparing a paper for drawing, shading forms, or holding his brush at the proper angle.

A mong Holbein's first works in Basel were illustrations for Erasmus's book, *Encomium moriae.* A preserved copy originally owned by the humanist Oswald Myconius (1488-1552) contains marginal drawings by the artist added in 1516. It is worth mentioning that Dürer also illustrated books while in Basel, including the highly popular *Das Narrenschiff* (The Ship of Fools) by the satiric poet Sebastian Brant (1457?-1494) and Erasmus's *Ritter vom Thurm.*

Shortly after arriving in Basel, Holbein received his first commission as a painter; for the knight Hans Baer he decorated a tabletop with scenes of hunting, tournaments, and birds and fish being caught.[6] At around the same time he did a signboard for Myconius, painted on both sides, and portraits of Jakob Meyer and his wife Dorothea.

After two years in Basel, Holbein moved to Lucerne; its mayor, Jakob von Hertenstein, had a new house whose facade and rooms needed decorating. Holbein completed this commission in under three years. Among the paintings were a number of portraits of Hertenstein's family, unified with meticulously executed ornamentation. This type of ornamentation made its first appearance in Middle European painting on two altar wings done by Holbein the Elder from 1508 to 1510 for the church of St. Ottilie in Hohenberg (illustration 1); today they may be seen in the National Gallery in Prague. The ornamentation for Hertenstein's house shows a more mature bearing, however, which leads one to suspect that Holbein the Younger paid a visit to Italy before starting to work. The twentieth-century scholar Paul Ganz tried to recreate this journey on the basis of evidence found in Holbein's paintings. He posits that the artist may have gone from Lucerne to Lugano to study the portal of the church San Lorenzo, and from there to Milan, Padua, Monza and Bergamo. The last report on the painter's sojourn in Lucerne is dated May 21, 1519.

By the summer of 1519 Holbein was back in Basel. He had returned to take care of his late brother Ambrosius's estate and to be nearer to his father, who was working in Benheim. The Basel artists' guild now recognized him as a master. Holbein once again set about illustrating books and did a number of woodcuts for title pages for volumes printed by Froben. A particularly beautiful example depicting the Virgin Mary and two saints dates back to this stage in his career; it was destined for the front page of the charter of Freiburg.

In 1521 Holbein began painting the Great Council Chamber of Basel's town hall. Less than a year before he had been named a burgher, an honor to which he obviously attached great importance; in 1543, after more than a decade of living in England, he would add "Citizen of Basel" to his name on a self-portrait. His task in the town hall was to cover the walls of the assembly room with allegorical figures, pictures of historical personalities, and scenes from classical history and mythology, setting them all in the midst of painted architecture.

He interrupted his work in the autumn and did not resume it until the summer of the following year. The reason for this hiatus is not known. Perhaps the artist was dissatisfied with his progress; perhaps he was distracted by the conflicts that had arisen among the city fathers over the Reformation; perhaps he had tired of the hall's poor illumination. Another decisive factor may have been that the theme, purely didactic in nature, had been determined in advance. Beatus Rhenanus had proposed it: O VOS REGENTES OBLITI PRIVATORUM PUBLICA CURATE (O aldermen, forget your private affairs and tend to public ones!). In addition, Holbein's figures and compositions were restricted by the overly accentuated frames. Toward the end of 1522 he gave up altogether, leaving the front wall empty; he would not draft this remaining space until 1530. The city council nevertheless paid his entire fee of 120 gulden.

In the months when he was not working on the town hall, Holbein produced drafts for painted windows. He also completed more book illustrations, the most notable among these being artistic paraphrases of Bible stories which were subsequently published in Martin Luther's translation. Around 1523 he began designing a series of 41 woodcuts entitled *Danse Macabre* (The Dance of Death) in which he evoked dreadful old pictures from the Middle Ages on the vanity of human endeavor. Here, surprisingly, he turned away from his customary orientation toward Italian modeling and imitated the style of the fifteenth-century German graphic artists.

He may have adopted this uncharacteristic Gothic stance as a protest against what was going on around him. Protestantism had been gaining considerably in strength and importance; Holbein was observing at close hand the emigration of large numbers of Catholics to the other side of the Rhine, and at one point Catholics were forced from the Basel city council. Neither the artist nor his friend Erasmus fell in with the Reformation. The turmoil inspired Holbein to contemplate human fate; the mystical appearance of his Bible illustrations and

*Danse Macabre* woodcuts may well have resulted from such deep thinking. Clearly his work was changing.

By 1526 the political scene in Basel had worsened considerably. Iconoclastic riots, censorship of the press, and what amounted to a freezing of the arts had created an environment that must have been intolerable for Holbein. After collecting the money owed him and settling his brother's estate, he left for England by way of the Netherlands, bearing letters of introduction from Erasmus.

T he first letter, dated August 19, 1526, was addressed to Peter Aegidius, the town clerk of Antwerp and proofreader for one of its leading printers. It gained Holbein admission to the studio of the painter Quentin Massys (1466?-1530). Another source informs us that Holbein had arrived in England by early September. He was now twenty-eight years old.

He was drawn toward London, the seat of Henry VIII, who had worn the crown since 1509. The news had spread that Henry was a king who governed by humanistic principles; soon after his coronation, Lord Montjoy had written to Erasmus, "O my dear Erasmus, if you could only see how pleased everybody here is. Our ruler does not aspire to gold, jewels, and precious metals; he seeks virtue, honor, and immortality."

Holbein's first work in England was probably a life-size portrait of Sir Thomas More (1478-1535), dated 1527. It had not taken long for the artist to win the favor of More, then Guardian of the Treasure of the Crown and a member of the king's privy council; he was entertained at More's house in Chelsey, not far from London. Erasmus was also a friend to the man who would be named lord chancellor of England in 1529 and beheaded in 1535 at the order of the king. Erasmus had written *Encomium moriae* in 1509 at More's home in Bucklesbury and dedicated it to his host. More himself was the author of numerous books, among them *Utopia*; the Swiss edition was published in Basel in 1518 by Froben and illustrated with woodcuts by the Holbein brothers.

Holbein also painted a large group portrait of More and his family. Although the original work has been lost, three copies of it have been preserved along with seven preliminary studies, including "Judge John More, Sir Thomas More's Father" (plate III), "John More, Sir Thomas More's Son" (plate XVII), "Anne Cresacre, Bride of John More, Age 16" (plate XVIII), and "Elisabeth Dauncey," daughter to Sir Thomas (plate XXI).

Portraits of More's friends — humanists, scholars and courtiers — followed. Visitors to the house in Chelsey may have witnessed Holbein painting any one of a number of personages: Sir Henry Guildford, a friend of the king and curator of the royal household who was awarded the Order of the Garter in 1527; William Warham, Archbishop of Canterbury, who was also decorated by the king and had previously served the Crown under Henry VII; Bishop John Fisher (the original portrait is no longer extant, but there is a copy of it dated 1528); Sir Henry Wyatt; Nikolaus Kratzer, the astronomer from Munich who was also in the king's service and taught More's daughter; and an unknown lady who probably belonged to the family circle. During this period Holbein never received an order directly from the king, although he had recommendations from both More and Archbishop Warham.

In 1528 Holbein returned to Basel and was admitted, after some hesitation, to the now official Protestant faith. His financial circumstances were such that he was able to buy a house on August 29 in the suburb of St. Johan. In 1520 he had wed the widow of the tanner Ulrich Schmid; she was four years older than he and probably brought considerable property of her own to the marriage. Their house was in the vicinity of the printer Froben's establishment, and Holbein doubtless looked forward to working with him again.

He had not reckoned on the continuing divisive impact of the Reformation. On Good Friday of 1528, a mob hauled the paintings out of St. Martin's church, and on the Monday following Easter did the same to the Augustinian church. The city council subsequently resolved to rid all the reformed churches of their religious works.

In what appears to have been a countermeasure, the chaplain of the Basel cathedral asked Holbein to paint new wings for the organ. The artist set to work immediately and completed his commission before further rioting broke out. In 1529 the town hall was once again rent by controversy. Armed bands raided still more churches, carrying away the pictures of the saints. In the cathedral, another target, the statues were smashed, but Holbein's freshly painted organ wings were left untouched because they were mounted too high to reach. A letter from Erasmus to their mutual friend Willibald Pirkheimer (1470-1530) reported that another of his works was destroyed.

By paying bribes, Holbein was able to save some of the pictures he had done for churches, but the city of Basel would never be the same. In just three days a wealth of artworks collected over a century had been lain to waste. Holbein was to suffer additional personal misfortunes. Not long after, the city council decreed that any further church and religious painting would be met with severe penalties. During this period, the artist was also deprived of the opportunity to work for his Basel book publishers, Froben among them.

Together with his friends Erasmus, Jakob Meyer and Hans Oberreid, Holbein remained true to the old faith. Some of his acquaintances, unwilling to retire from public life, moved to Freiburg. Despite the fact that his chances of winning large commissions were slim, Holbein stayed on in Basel, living off of his savings. In 1531 he bought a farmstead at nearby Fischern.

S ometime between 1528 and 1532 Holbein painted a portrait of his wife and their two sons. This is the only picture from his entire known oeuvre in which his personal feelings are evident. His wife's worried features and the tear-stained, serious faces of his children express his own sorrow at the hopeless position in which he found himself and his concern for his family's future.

His situation gradually improved. With the help of Heinrich Petri, he got in touch with the scientist Sebastian Münster (1489-1552) and agreed to do woodcut illustrations for Münster's *Cosmographia Universa*, the first detailed description of the world in German, and for an essay on astronomy. It is possible that he had previously been recommended to Münster by Nikolaus Kratzer, whose portrait he had painted while in England. Thanks to other new patrons, Holbein finally received a commission from the Basel city council. In 1530 he was invited back to the town hall to paint the wall he had left blank in 1522; for his efforts he received 60 gulden. He also traveled to Freiburg to paint Erasmus.

The city council subsequently paid him another 14 gulden for work done on the Rhine Gate, a painted sun clock; during the winter of 1531 he worked for Münster again. Apparently these and other projects were not enough, for in 1532 he returned to London. He spent his remaining 11 years in England, leaving his family behind in Basel; he never returned to Switzerland to live.

I mmediately upon arriving in England, Holbein found himself in worse circumstances than those he had fled from at home. Thomas More had fallen into disgrace with the king and lived in seclusion in the country. He had refused to swear an oath on Henry VIII's sovereignty over the church and resigned his position as lord chancellor. In spite of warnings from his friend the Duke of Norfolk ("The king's disgrace means death"), More persevered in declaring that he "first served God and then his prince"; not to be corrupted, he returned all the presents Henry had given him along with his seal of office. The friendship he had previously enjoyed with the king was over.

When More also refused to uphold the king's divorce from Catherine of Aragon and failed to attend Anne Boleyn's coronation, Henry was furious. In April of 1534 More was imprisoned in the Tower of London; in July of 1535 he was sentenced to death by hanging, commuted by the king to decapitation. He was executed on July 6 and his head was fixed upon the London Bridge.

Archbishop Warham, too, had incurred the king's wrath, but his death by natural causes in 1532 saved him from more severe punishment. It also prevented him from witnessing firsthand how Henry VIII, initially a strong defender of the Catholic church against Martin Luther, had turned against it when the pope would not grant him a divorce from Catherine. Warham was already dead by the time Holbein reached England.

The artist had to develop new connections. He looked toward the Hanseatic League, an organization of German merchants and shipowners who had established a colony at the Steel Yard in London. The members of the Hanse soon began to order portraits from Holbein, the majority of which have been preserved. Two goldsmiths, Hans of Antwerp and Hans of Zurich, commissioned him to design metal goblets, pitchers and plates. Technical skill, versatility and a fertile imagination allowed Holbein to take on such unusual work. He won the respect of his patrons, who directed other orders from their guild his way; Holbein painted for them two large depictions of triumphant processions.[7]

In May of 1533 he painted a picture celebrating the arrival of Anne Boleyn in England, and four years later he officially entered the service of Henry VIII. The French poet Nicholas Bourbon, who earlier had written accompanying verses for Holbein's *Danse Macabre* cycle, dubbed him the "royal painter and Appelles of our time" (Appelles was the fourth-century court painter of Philip of Macedon and Alexander the Great). Holbein remained a "servant of His Royal Highness" in the full sense of the word until his death.

His commissions for the king included a large fresco including the impressive figures of Henry, his queen at the time and, on a raised step in the background, his parents, Henry VII and Elizabeth of York. An index of Holbein's extant works lists portraits of the queens Anne Boleyn, Jane Seymour, Anne of Cleves and the unfortunate Catherine Howard. He also painted princes, landed gentry and the king himself. Holbein's most famous portrait of Henry VIII shows the monarch presenting the Decree of Freedom to the guild of barbers and surgeons. Here the king appears far larger and grander than the other people depicted. He stands at the front, looking out of the picture, with his legs imperiously apart — like a god of the ancient Orient. Clearly Holbein was doing his best to keep Henry happy. In addition to works officially ordered by the court, he also did portraits of scientists, unknown citizens and other artists of the time.

While at court, Holbein reaped the benefits of his elevated

position. He was admired and covered with all the glory a sixteenth-century painter could possibly desire. The king even sent him to the continent several times to paint pictures of people he wanted to meet. On March 12, 1538, for example, Hans was in Brussels drawing the widow of the Duke of Milan, who had been recommended to Henry as a possible spouse. In August he traveled to Burgundy and Lyons; from Lyons he took a short side trip to Basel, where his family still lived. A contemporary, Dr. Ludwig Iselm, wrote to Bonifacius Amerbach about this visit and reported that Holbein had been dressed in velvets and silks.

The Basel city council wanted him to stay. They promised to pay him a regular salary as a building consultant for which he would have no further obligations; they also offered to transfer his salary to his wife if he remained in Basel for at least two years. It seems, however, that Holbein's loyalties now rested with Henry VIII. He returned to London, taking his son Philip with him, and apprenticed the boy to the Parisian goldsmith David.

In 1539 Holbein made another journey to the continent, this time to paint Anne and Amalie, the daughters of the Duke of Cleves, at Düren Castle. One year later Henry married Anne. Holbein continued to work for the king until his unexpected death in 1543 in a London plague epidemic. Only forty-six years old, he was in the midst of working on a large painting for Barbes Hall. The precise day he died is not known; nor is the site of his burial.

Shortly before, Holbein had found the time to draft a will in the presence of some friends. He may well have feared for his life; in the sixteenth century there was almost nothing one could do in the face of a plague. His will — in which he Anglicized the spelling of his name and that of the goldsmith Hans of Antwerp — reads as follows:

> In the name of the Father, the Son, and the Holy Ghost, I, John Holbein, servant of His Majesty the King, make this disposition and last will that my property shall be sold, including my horse, and I wish that my debts shall be paid, especially to Mr. Anthony, the King's servant in Greenwich, in the amount of 10 pounds, 13 shillings, and 7 pence sterling. I wish further that he shall be relieved of all obligations that exist between him and me. I also owe 6 pounds sterling to Mr. John of Antwerp, the goldsmith, and I wish that he shall get paid together with the first debt. I further assign 7 shillings and 6 pence sterling monthly for the support of my two children who are in foster care. To confirm this I affix my seal, and this my disposition of October seven in the year of the Lord 1543 is sealed by the witnesses: Anthony Secher, ordnance blacksmith; Mr. John of Antwerp, abovementioned goldsmith; Ulrich Obynger, merchant; and Harry Maynert, painter.[8]

L ittle else is known about the life of Hans Holbein the Younger. Not one note or letter from his own hand survives and his personality remains an enigma. Even the people who knew him left conflicting opinions. Erasmus, for example, alternately praised him and denounced him as opportunistic.

Given the sheer quantities of work he produced, we may assume that he had scant time for a frenzied or complicated private life. The labor-intensive nature of his calling bound him to his studio; the technical requirements of his art necessitated that he focus on it to the exclusion of other concerns. He may have deliberately avoided the public eye, and it is certain that he did not invite its scrutiny by painting elaborate self-portraits. The only surviving authentic self-portrait is in fact a miniature from 1543, which bears the artist's initials and age (45) at the time.

We must turn to Holbein's art for a picture of the man; if we examine it closely, we can see the character of his consciousness. We can also learn much about the world in which he lived. The social standing of his portrait subjects enable us to divide Holbein's oeuvre into three groups, which, interestingly, correspond with the three stages of his artistic development.

If we discount his early works, done under his father's supervision at their home in Augsburg, we may begin with his Basel period, dominated by works made for citizens or donated by citizens and intended for the local churches. Included in this is his series of portrayals of Basel humanists, which would later be followed by his portraits of English humanists. His permanent stay in London may be broken into two periods: the first, when he painted the merchants and the members of the royal court; and the final, when the demands of King Henry VIII predominated.

During his Basel period Holbein created religious works as well as portraits. Some pieces combine both elements of his creative activity. For example, when he painted altar wings in Frieburg he included the family of his patron, the merchant Hans Oberreid; the scenes of the adoration of the shepherds and the magi are positioned above two portrait groups. In his famous painting *The Virgin with the Family of Burgomaster Jakob Meyer*, Mary's revelation is incongruously combined with portrait-like renditions of Meyer family members. The burgomaster himself, incidentally, had a rather spotted reputation; he reportedly acquired his properties through speculation, reckless business transactions, and two advantageous marriages. Holbein, however, depicted him as a humble petitioner whom the Virgin has taken under her protective cloak.

This work may also be seen as a sort of sociopolitical commentary: in the ideal world — the one the humanists sought — the son of a grocer could occupy a place formerly reserved for crowned heads. Since 1499, Basel's nobility had had almost no influence within the city. Rulers were elected from among guild memberships, and the city council was supposed to direct all resolutions toward the benefit of the citizenry.[9]

*The Virgin with the Family of Burgomaster Jakob Meyer* contains other meanings that may be deduced from the composition of the kneeling women at right. The Virgin's face is turned toward them. Meyer's first wife, who had died some time before the painting was made, is next to her and appears to be looking out beyond the mortal world. Closer to the viewer is Dorothea Kannengiesser, Meyer's second wife. She seems different from the others and her gaze makes it clear that she is also separated from them spiritually; unlike her husband, she supported the Reformation.[10] Thematically this picture preserves the Middle Ages. The attention paid to clothing and fine details (for example, the beautiful Oriental carpet on which the group is placed)[11] is in strict adherence with the objectiveness of the Renaissance.

In Basel Holbein became the painter of citizens. He was himself a citizen, a member of the middle class whose ideology was based on humanism. Its central principles were human dignity, personal well-being and the pursuit of private interests. It argued against medieval feudal asceticism and elevated the individual's right to assert his or her personality above the obligation of self-renunciation. Holbein, with his classical ideal of pure form, was perfectly suited to the task of painting its leading figures.

He first painted Erasmus, the most important exponent of European humanism, in 1523. In the years to come he would complete five portraits of him, becoming his painter much as Lucas Cranach became Martin Luther's. As Erasmus himself tells us, he did not like sitting for portraits and usually only gave in to accommodate his friends. Not until he had seen Holbein's illustrations for *Encomium moriae*, and his picture of Bonifacius Amerbach, would he agree to sit for the artist from Augsburg. Prior to that, in 1517, he had been painted by the Dutch master Quentin Massys, and in 1520 Dürer had drawn him on his journey through the Netherlands.[12]

During his first sojourn in England Holbein was taken care of by another humanist, Thomas More, and came to know and paint the members of his circle. When he returned there in 1532 that circle had been destroyed by Henry VIII, who had gradually eliminated those who opposed him in the name of humanistic moral principles, which Henry then saw as tantamount to loyalty toward Rome. News of these developments may have reached Holbein in Antwerp, where he stopped on his way to London. He likely knew before reaching England that More had resigned and Warham was ill (or dead), and that the king was intensifying his fight against the old church. Unable to count on his former clientele, it made sense for him to go to the Steel Yard, the seat of the German Hanse in England. It seems that Erasmus got word of the artist's actions and did not approve; in one of his letters dating from the period, he noted that "in England [Holbein] disappointed those to whom he had been recommended."[13]

The Hanse had been active in London since the twelfth century. From their guild hall near London Bridge, its members worked to guard their international trading interests. They formed a tight colony and lived according to the customs of their homeland, which may have been another reason Holbein grew close to them. In 1532 he did three portraits of Hanse members, of which *Portrait of the Merchant Georg Gisze*, now in the Berlin Museum, is probably the most famous. He succeeded in capturing the cool, self-assured matter-of-factness characteristic of these powerful merchants. Obviously he also befriended some of them; he painted Hans of Antwerp several times and made him an executor of his will. Other portraits from those days, some of which are known only from copies, include personalities from the vicinity of Henry VIII's court, notably General George Neville, Sir Henry Guildford, Reskimer of Murthyr, and the poet Henry Howard.

A study of these portraits reveals Holbein's concerns at this stage. Often an entire picture is taken up by a face, which fills the frame like a kind of relief; the artist was no longer interested in working out the details of a subject's surroundings. He may have been conscious of recording history; on many drawings we find golden inscriptions giving the individual's name and age and the year in which the portrait was done.

Holbein first painted King Henry VIII in 1536. Soon afterward he was proclaimed court painter and allocated a salary of 30 pounds per year. His inaugural commission in the king's service was a double portrait of Henry and his current queen, Jane Seymour. The king had a reputation for being a vigorous, inconsiderate ruler, a passionate hunter who could stay in the saddle for days, and a brutal wrestler; Holbein depicted him as an author of verses and player of the lute. In this painting Henry's expression conveys kindness, good humor and friendliness toward people.

The work Holbein devoted to the king, his wives and members of his court is notable for its austere style, which may be seen as a metaphor for the nature of his relationship with his subjects. Only the king is repeatedly portrayed as he appeared to his court, when he showed up: enlivened by wine and heavily perfumed, he went among them to prove anew that he was the best-dressed monarch of his time and represented the richest court in Europe. Holbein spent the rest of his life in this milieu, leaving it only once, in 1538, to work briefly for the Hanse.

The drawings of Hans Holbein the Younger communicate a unified message rare in the history of art. They evidence his lifelong search for objective truth and testify both to his will and his exceptional artistic talents and abilities. As we study them we realize how timeless they are; in many respects they appear almost contemporary. Like his paintings, Holbein's drawings captured the essence of the Renaissance.

The drawings have been preserved to an extent virtually unknown for any other artist of that era. The majority are housed in two collections, both of which originated in the artist's lifetime and have endured to this day. The first, in the Kunstmuseum in Basel, contains drawings from Holbein's years in that city and was begun by Bonifacius Amerbach, one of his patrons there. In 1578 Holbein's son Basileos drew up a list of the 74 drawings in Amerbach's estate and added to it those that had been kept by his own family. The second collection, now at Windsor Castle and numbering 80 portraits, includes the drawings found in Holbein's studio at Whitehall after his death. Because the artist died in the king's service, the drawings remained in the possession of the royal family.

The Windsor Castle collection arrived there via a rather circuitous route. The first known recorded evidence of its existence dates back to the year 1590, when the drawings were held by Lord Lumley, although the source emphasizes that they previously belonged to King Edward VI (1537-1553). In the seventeenth century they had found their way into the hands of Thomas, Fourteenth Earl of Arundel (1585?-1646), one of the first large-scale collectors of art in England and a patron of the Bohemian artist Wenceslaus Hollar (1607-1677), who copied some of them. Following the earl's death the collection was returned to the royal family, then headed by the Stuart king Charles I. In 1727, after the crowning of George II, the drawings were found in a chest at Kensington Castle. Two centuries old and well traveled, they were in need of restoration; Queen Caroline saw to it. The drawings were thoroughly cleaned, lines which had become almost illegible were meticulously retraced, and the collection was hung on the walls at Castle Richmond Lodge. Later it was moved back to Kensington Castle; during the eighteenth century Francesco Bartolozzi (1727-1815) used the drawings as models for some of his engravings.

The Kunstmuseum collection is the richer in terms of subject matter; it contains studies for compositions of larger panel and wall paintings, drafts for goldsmiths' works, models for painters of church windows and for metalworkers, drafts for woodcarvers, and perspective and decoration studies as well as portraits. The Windsor Castle collection contains only portraits, with one exception: a drawing of King Solomon and the Queen of Sheba. The reproductions in this volume represent a selection of the most famous and artistically significant drawings from both the Basel and London holdings.

Today Holbein's drawings are prized as highly as his paintings, and not only because our perception of the value of drawing has changed. Perhaps because he did them for himself, as tools to be used later, they constitute a freer expression of his gift. Their brilliance has never been questioned; they remain unsurpassed in the history of art.

A Holbein drawing gleams with quiet beauty. Its focus is most often the human face set against a background devoid of detail; the face bears little or no expression. The subject is portrayed with total objectivity. There is no indication of his or her character or personality, or of any relationship with the artist; there is virtually no content to distract us. It is as if Holbein worked with utter coolness, detached from the people who sat for him and indifferent to them as individuals. He was interested only in what he saw. In that respect he resembled the scientists of his epoch, who renounced medieval notions, studied reality, and thereby discovered its laws.

Holbein's preference for the techniques of the Italian Renaissance determined his own working methods. His earlier studies (plates XXV, XLI, and XLII) were done with silverpoint on soft handmade paper. So the paper would hold the color, he treated its surface with a solution of gum arabic mixed with bone meal. Colored drawings were usually done with red chalk or pen and ink; in some instances color was laid on later (plates I and X). Occasionally he drew on paper he had previously colored (plate XXXVIII). Rust-brown ink was sometimes used on uppermost lines to achieve a better differentiation from the foundation (plates XXVII, XXIX, XXXII, and XL). As artists had done since the end of the fifteenth century, Holbein fixed his drawings when they were finished with a process Dürer had brought to Germany from Italy.

The later drawings (plate XXXV) reflect the influence of the French Renaissance artist Jean Clouet (1485?-1545), who himself had been influenced by Leonardo da Vinci. But while Clouet's system of drawing was stylized, Holbein's was looser and more free. The different ways in which the two men worked are evident from the drawings each did of the French envoy Jean de Dinteville. Holbein painted him twice: one picture shows him with his friend Georges de Seive; the other, *The Man with the Lute*, is in the Berlin Museum. The drawing reproduced in this volume (plate XXXIV) is identical to neither of these, but scholars believe it depicts the same man. It is housed in the Windsor Castle collection. Compared with Clouet's drawing in Castle Chantilly, it is far livelier; the skin, the hair and the beard look natural and the eyes are vivid. While Clouet's drawing may be more masterly than Holbein's, it is less realistic.

Holbein frequently captured a face on the first attempt. It was not unusual for him to use a single neutral study in several paintings, fitting it into each prepared composition. Thus it is possible that the study of Jakob Meyer

30

(plate XXXV) was initially used for the portrait completed in 1516 and again, ten years later, for *The Virgin with the Family of Burgomaster Jakob Meyer*.

He sometimes left a drawing virtually unchanged when incorporating it into a painting or a final portrait. At other times he altered one or more elements. For example, the study of Meyer's daughter Anna (plate XXXVII) shows her sitting with her hands lying quietly in her lap; in the portrait, she is a woman absorbed by her prayer.

Whatever the outcome, however, the human face was always Holbein's starting point and primary concern. When he painted Thomas More's family, for example, he began by drawing each head individually (plates III, XVII, XVIII, and XXI). He then did a sketch of the entire portrait. In this sketch, which has been preserved, it is evident that he was not yet thinking too hard about the end result; he was still intent on precisely capturing each person's appearance. Only when he was satisfied with this portion of his work did he draft the entire group in the setting in which it would ultimately be placed.

At times he drew nothing but a face (plate XXV), or a face accompanied by the merest suggestion of clothing and body position, as in his preliminary study for a portrait of Sir Nicholas Carew (plate XXII). In the final portrait of Carew, Holbein paid an unusual amount of attention to the splendid armor, the rich fabric curtain in the background and the posture of his subject, who holds a sword and pennant in his hands.

We find few detail studies among Holbein's artistic bequest. Occasionally he sketched a detail or two on a portrait drawing (plates XII and XXVI) or prepared an important part of a future painting separately (plate XLIII). The hands are those of Erasmus.

The composition studies included in this volume (plates XLV-L) reveal another facet of Holbein's talent. For these he relied mainly on his imagination, adopting from reality only what he was able to transfer in its pure form. In this he was pursuing an objective also sought by Leonardo da Vinci, who noted in *Trattato della Pittura* that drawing dealt with an endless number of things nature did not produce, not just those it did. Holbein's composition studies were produced mainly as models for decorative paintings or book illustrations.

The final five drawings in our selection (plates LIII-LVII) were once believed to be the work of Hans Holbein the Younger; they no longer are. We offer them here as examples of his influence on his contemporaries.

# NOTES

1. Bushart, Bruno, *Hans Holbein der Ältere* (Bonn: Inter Nationes, 1965).

2. Grohn, Hans Werner, *Hans Holbein der Jüngere als Maler* (Leipzig: VEB E.A. Seemann Verlag, 1955), page 15.

3. Durus, Alfred, "Hans Holbein der Jüngere und Erasmus von Rotterdam," *Forum* I/5, pages 16 ff.

4. The first landscape drawing of the Renaissance, dated August 5, 1473, is a work by Leonardo da Vinci. It was not until the early sixteenth century that landscape painting attained an important position in European art. Then, despite plagues, peasants' revolts and religious conflicts, many artists traveled throughout Europe to add to their store of knowledge and sketch from nature.

5. The development of landscape motifs in sixteenth-century German painting was strongly influenced by Dutch painters, in particular Joachim Patinir (1485?-1524). Holbein's *Allegory of the Old and the New Testament*, with a landscape in the background, may be the most obvious proof of this influence.

6. Vögelin, Salomon, *Der Holbeintisch in der Stadtbibliothek in Zürich* (Wien: 1878).

7. In 1934 the Holbein scholar Hans Koegler published a report, "Jahresbericht der Öffentlichen Kunstsammlung, Basel," saying that both pictures probably belonged to the Olmütz Archbishop Karl Lichtenstein.

8. Grohn, p. 43.

9. Wackernagel, Rudolf, *Humanismus and Reformation*, volume 3 of *Geschichte der Stadt Basel* (Basel: 1924).

10. Grohn, pp. 21-22.

11. The oriental carpets which appear in Holbein's works are mentioned in Fierrero, M.V., *Teppiche* (Munich: Südwest-Verlag, 1971) as "Holbein-type."

12. Grohn, p. 19.

13. Ganz, Paul, *Zwei Werke Hans Holbein der Jüngere aus der Fruhzeit des ersten englischen Aufenthalts*, a commemorative publication for the opening of the Kunstmuseum (Basel: 1936), pp. 141 ff.

# SELECTED BIBLIOGRAPHY

*Die Malerfamilie Holbein*, ed. Hans Reinhardt and Georg Schmidt; catalogue by Erwin Treu, Paul-Henry Boerlin, Hanspeter Landolt, Margarethe Pfister-Burkhalter, Hans Reinhardt, Catherine Schindler, and Alfred Wys. Catalogue for the 1960 exhibition at the Kunstmuseum in Basel (Basel, 1960).

*Holbein and His Contemporaries.* (John Herron Art Museum, 1950). Illustrated exhibition catalogue.

Chamberlain, Arthur Bensley. *Holbein, Hans the Younger* (New York: Dodd, Mead & Company, 1913).

Chamberlain, John. *Imitations of Original Drawings by Hans Holbein in the Collection of His Majesty, for the Portraits of Illustrious Persons of the Court of Henry VIII* (1812).

Ganz, Paul. *Die Handzeichnungen Hans Holbein dem Jüngeren, Mappen mit kirtischem Katalog* (Berlin, 1937).

—*Die Handzeichnungen von Hans Holbein dem Jüngeren in Auswahl* (Berlin, 1937).

Glaser, Curt. *Hans Holbein der Jüngere, Zeichnungen* ⸝Basel, 1924).

Grohn, H.W. *Hans Holbein der Jüngere, Bildniszeichnungen* (Dresden, 1956).

Holmes, Richard. *Hans Holbeins Bildnisse von Berühmten Persönlichkeiten nach den auf der Bibliothek zu Windsor befindlichen Handzeichnungen* (Munich, 1895).

Lofts, Norah. *Anne Boleyn* (New York: Coward, McCann & Geoghegan, Inc., 1979).

Parker, K.T. *The Drawings of Holbein at Windsor Castle* (Oxford and London, 1945).

Reinhardt, Hans. *Holbein.* (Paris: Hyperion Press, 1938). Translated from the French by Prudence Montagu-Pollock.

Scheffler, K. *Dessins de Hans Holbein le Jeune* (Paris, 1944).

Schmid, H.A. *Hans Holbein der Jüngere, sein Aufstieg zur Meisterschaft und sein englischer Stil* (Basel, 1948).

Waetzoldt, W. *Hans Holbein der Jüngere, Bildnisse, 24 farbige handzeichnungen* (Leipzig and Wiesbaden, 1954).

Williams, Neville. *Henry VII and His Court* (New York: The Macmillan Company, 1971).

# CATALOGUE

—Cover—

SIR JOHN GODSALVE
*(see plate X)*


—Frontispiece —

KING HENRY VIII
*(see plate VI)*


# ILLUSTRATIONS IN TEXT


—Page 5—

HANS HOLBEIN THE ELDER: ALTAR WINGS WITH ST. BARBARA,
ST. APPOLLONIA, ST. ROCHUS AND ST. OTTILIE
*135 x 79 cm.*
*Prague, The National Gallery*


—Page 7—

HANS HOLBEIN THE YOUNGER: LADY VAUX
*Tempera on wood*
*36.5 x 27 cm.*
*Prague, The National Gallery*


—Page 9—

HANS HOLBEIN THE ELDER: PORTRAIT OF THE ARTIST'S CHILDREN,
AMBROSIUS AND HANS, 1511
*10.3 x 15.5 cm.*
*Basel, Kupferstichkabinett, Kunstmuseum*

# THE PLATES

## —I—

### PORTRAIT OF AN UNKNOWN MAN, *ca.* 1537
*Colored chalks completed by opaque colors, 37.2 x 30.4 cm.*
*(Once thought to be a self-portrait)*
*Basel, Kupferstichkabinett, Kunstmuseum*

## —II—

### THEOPHRASTUS BOMBASTUS OF HOHENHEIM, CALLED PARACELSUS
*Colored chalks, slightly washed, 40.1 x 36.6 cm.*
*Basel, Kupferstichkabinett, Kunstmuseum*

## —III—

### JUDGE JOHN MORE, SIR THOMAS MORE'S FATHER
*Chalk drawing, 35.4 x 27.6 cm.*
*(Study for the group portrait of Thomas More's family from 1526-1527)*
*Windsor, Windsor Castle*

## —IV—

### WILLIAM WARHAM, ARCHBISHOP OF CANTERBURY
*Chalk drawing, colored, 40.7 x 30.9 cm.*
*(Study for the portrait from 1527 now in the Lambeth Palace in London;*
*portions have been retraced)*
*Windsor, Windsor Castle*

## —V—

### CARDINAL FISHER, BISHOP OF ROCHESTER (1535)
*Chalk and pen drawing, slightly colored, 38.3 x 23.4 cm.*
*Windsor, Windsor Castle*

## —VI—

### KING HENRY VIII (1537)
*Brush drawing on canvas*
*(Detail from a cartoon; cartoon dimensions 258.7 x 135 cm.)*
*London, National Gallery*

—VII—

KING HENRY VII (1537)
*Brush drawing on canvas*
*(Detail from a cartoon; same as above)*
*London, National Gallery*


—VIII—

SIR THOMAS WYATT, POET AND DIPLOMAT AT THE COURT OF KING HENRY VIII
*Colored chalks, 37 x 27 cm.*
*(Probably a preliminary drawing for the portrait from 1537)*
*Windsor, Windsor Castle*


—IX—

SIR HENRY GUILDFORD, EQUERRY OF KING HENRY VIII
*Colored chalks, partly washed, 38.5 x 29.5 cm.*
*(Study for the portrait from 1527)*
*Windsor, Windsor Castle*


—X—

SIR JOHN GODSALVE
*Colored chalks, colored afterward, 36.4 x 29.3 cm.*
*(Study for the portrait from 1536)*
*Windsor, Windsor Castle*


—XI—

PHILIP HOBBY, PRIVY COUNCILLOR FOR KING HENRY VIII
*Chalk drawing, 30 x 22.2 cm.*
*(Study for the portrait)* 12×9
*Windsor, Windsor Castle*


—XII—

WILLIAM PARR, MARQUIS OF NORTHAMPTON
*Chalk and pen drawing, slightly colored, 31.7 x 21.2 cm.*
*Windsor, Windsor Castle*

39

—XIII—

## SIR GEORGE CAREW, WHO DIED IN 1545 IN A SHIPWRECK
*Chalk drawing, slightly colored, 31.7 x 25.3 cm.*
*Windsor, Windsor Castle*


—XIV—

## JOHN POYNS OF ESSEX
*Chalk drawing, slightly washed, 29.5 x 23.3 cm.*
*Windsor, Windsor Castle*


—XV—

## EDWARD CLINTON, COUNT OF LINCOLN
*Colored chalks, 22.2 x 14.4 cm.*
*(Study for the portrait)*
*Windsor, Windsor Castle*


—XVI—

## SIR RICHARD SOUTHWELL
*Chalk drawing, 36.8 x 27.8 cm.*
*(Study for the portrait from 1536 now in the Uffizi;*
*portions have been retraced)*
*Windsor, Windsor Castle*


—XVII—

## JOHN MORE, SIR THOMAS MORE'S SON
*Chalk drawing, partly colored, 38 x 28 cm.*
*(Study for the group portrait of Thomas More's family from 1526-1527)*
*Windsor, Windsor Castle*


—XVIII—

## ANNE CRESACRE, BRIDE OF JOHN MORE, AGE SIXTEEN
*Black chalk, partly colored, 37.3 x 26.6 cm.*
*(Study for the group portrait of Thomas More's family from 1526-1527)*
*Windsor, Windsor Castle*

—XIX—

HENRY HOWARD, COUNT OF SURREY (1533)
*Chalk drawing, colored, 29 x 21 cm.*
*(Study for the portrait from 1541-1543)*
*Windsor, Windsor Castle*

—XX—

SIMON GEORGE OF CORNWALL
*Colored chalks, 28.1 x 19.3*
*(Study for the portrait from 1535)*
*Windsor, Windsor Castle*

—XXI—

ELISA'BETH DAUNCEY
*Colored chalks, partly washed and colored, 37.1 x 26.2 cm.*
*(Study for the group portrait of Thomas More's family from 1526-1527)*
*Windsor, Windsor Castle*

—XXII—

SIR NICHOLAS CAREW
*Colored chalks, 55 x 38 cm.*
*(Study for the portrait now at Drumlanrig Castle)*
*Basel, Kupferstichkabinett, Kunstmuseum*

—XXIII—

LADY MARY GUILDFORD
*Colored chalks, 55 x 38 cm.*
*(Study for the portrait from 1527)*
*Basel, Kupferstichkabinett, Kunstmuseum*

—XXIV—

LADY MARGARET ELIOT, WIFE OF SIR THOMAS
*Chalk drawing, partly colored, 27.7 x 20.6 cm.*
*Windsor, Windsor Castle*

—XXV—

**LADY BOROW**
*Chalk drawing, colored, 27.2 x 19.4 cm.*
*Windsor, Windsor Castle*


—XXVI—

**LADY RATCLIFF**
*Colored chalks, partly colored, 29.7 x 20 cm.*
*Windsor, Windsor Castle*


—XXVII—

**CATHERINE WILLOUGHBY DE GRESLY, FOURTH WIFE OF CHARLES BRANDON,
DUKE OF SUFFOLK**
*Colored chalks, partly colored, 29 x 21 cm.*
*Windsor, Windsor Castle*


—XXVIII—

**UNKNOWN LADY**
*Chalk drawing, 35.5 x 24.6 cm.*
*Windsor, Windsor Castle*


—XXIX—

**UNKNOWN LADY**
*Chalk and pen drawing, partly colored, 27 x 16.8 cm.*
*(Once thought to be a study for the portrait of Anne of Cleves,*
*fourth wife of Henry VIII, or of her sister Amalie;*
*portions have been retraced)*
*Windsor, Windsor Castle*


—XXX—

**UNKNOWN LADY**
*Chalk drawing, 27.5 x 24 cm.*
*Windsor, Windsor Castle*

## —XXXI—

**UNKNOWN LADY**
*Chalk drawing, 28.5 x 22.6 cm.*
*Windsor, Windsor Castle*


## —XXXII—

**UNKNOWN MAN**
*Chalk and pen drawing, 27.2 x 21 cm.*
*Windsor, Windsor Castle*


## —XXXIII—

**UNKNOWN MAN**
*Chalk drawing, 25.9 x 20.2 cm.*
*Windsor, Windsor Castle*

10 x 8

## —XXXIV—

**UNKNOWN MAN**
*(probably Jean de Dinteville)*
*Chalk drawing, partly colored, 40.5 x 29.4 cm.*
*Windsor, Windsor Castle*


## —XXXV—

**JAKOB MEYER, BURGOMASTER OF BASEL**
*Pencil and red ochre drawing, 28.1 x 19.1 cm.*
*(Study for the portrait from 1526)*
*Basel, Kupferstichkabinett, Kunstmuseum*


## —XXXVI—

**DOROTHEA MEYER, NÉE KANNENGIESSER**
*Colored chalks, partly washed, 39.5 x 28.2 cm.*
*(Study for the Madonna of Burgomaster Jakob Meyer from 1526-1530)*
*Basel, Kupferstichkabinett, Kunstmuseum*

## —XXXVII—

**ANNA MEYER, DAUGHTER OF JAKOB MEYER**
*Chalk drawing, partly colored, 39 x 27.5 cm.*
*(Study for the Madonna of Burgomaster Jakob Meyer from 1526-1530)*
*Basel, Kupferstichkabinett, Kunstmuseum*

## —XXXVIII—

**UNKNOWN LADY**
*Chalk drawing, colored, 26.2 x 18.2 cm.*
*Basel, Kupferstichkabinett, Kunstmuseum*

## —XXXIX—

**UNKNOWN LADY**
*Chalk drawing, partly colored, 40.2 x 29 cm.*
*Windsor, Windsor Castle*

## —XL—

**UNKNOWN MAN**
*(probably a member of the German Hanse)*
*Colored chalks and pen drawing, 32.1 x 23.9 cm.*
*Berlin, Kupferstichkabinett*

## —XLI—

**DUKE JEAN DE BERRY**
*Colored chalks, partly colored, 40 x 27 cm.*
*Basel, Kupferstichkabinett, Kunstmuseum*

## —XLII—

**JEANNE DE BOULOGNE, DUCHESS OF BERRY**
*Colored chalks, partly colored, 40 x 27 cm.*
*Basel, Kupferstichkabinett, Kunstmuseum*

## —XLIII—

### STUDY OF A HAND
*Brown chalk and red ochre, 20.5 x 15.2*
(Drawing for the portrait of Erasmus of Rotterdam from 1523)
Paris, The Louvre


## —XLIV—

### STUDY OF A LAMB
*India ink drawing, slightly toned, 20.6 x 24.6*
*Basel, Kupferstichkabinett, Kunstmuseum*


## —XLV—

### A MIDDLE-CLASS WOMAN OF BASEL
*Washed pen drawing, 29.1 x 19.9*
*Basel, Kupferstichkabinett, Kunstmuseum*


## —XLVI—

### STUDY OF A WOMAN OF BASEL
*Washed pen drawing, 25.4 x 19.7 cm.*
*Basel, Kupferstichkabinett, Kunstmuseum*


## —XLVII—

### THREE PEASANTS
*Washed pen drawing, 41.5 x 30.1 cm.*
*Basel, Kupferstichkabinett, Kunstmuseum*


## —XLVIII—

### SAILING SHIP ON DEPARTURE
*Pen drawing, colored, 40.4 x 51.8 cm.*
*Frankfurt/Main, Städel's Art Institut*

## —XLIX—

### FIGHTING LANSQUENETS
*Washed pen drawing, 28.4 x 43.4 cm.*
*Basel, Kupferstichkabinett, Kunstmuseum*

## —L—

### FIVE MUSICIANS IN THE GALLERY
*Washed pen drawing, 13 x 18.2 cm.*
*London, The British Museum*

## —LI—

### UNKNOWN MAN
*Colored chalks, colored, and red ochre, 41 x 34.2 cm.*
*(Once thought to be a self-portrait of the artist at age 26)*
*Basel, Kupferstichkabinett, Kunstmuseum*

## —LII—

### STUDY OF A YOUNG WOMAN, MODEL FOR THE MADONNA OF SOLOTHURN
*Pen and red ochre drawing, 19.7 x 16.5 cm.*
*(Ordered by the Basel town clerk Gerster in 1522)*
*Paris, The Louvre*

## RELATED WORKS
The following were once attributed to Hans Holbein the Younger.

## —LIII—

### HANS HOLBEIN THE ELDER: MADONNA
*Silver and white chalk drawing, 14 x 11.2 cm.*
*(Paul Ganz attributed this drawing to Hans Holbein the Younger;*
*later it was thought to be the work of his brother Ambrosius;*
*since the 1960 exhibition in Basel, "Die Malerfamilie Holbein" [The Holbeins:*
*A Family of Painters] it has been attributed to Hans Holbein the Elder*
*and is listed in connection with his "Böhler Madonna.")*
*Basel, Kupferstichkabinett, Kunstmuseum*

—LIV—

**UNKNOWN ARTIST: KING HENRY VIII**
*Chalk drawing, partly colored, 31 x 25 cm.*
*(Believed to be a copy from the sixteenth century)*
*Munich, Graphic Collection*


—LV—

**UNKNOWN ARTIST: CATHERINE WILLOUGHBY DE GRESLY**
*Washed chalk, later completed by pastel and pen drawing, 29.1 x 20.7 cm.*
*(Copy from Holbein's original; cf. plate XXVII)*
*London, The British Museum*


—LVI—

**UNKNOWN ARTIST: PORTRAIT OF A YOUNG MAN (1524-1526)**
*Colored chalks, partly washed, 21.1 x 19.6 cm.*
*Budapest, Szépmüvészeti Museum*


—LVII—

**UNKNOWN ARTIST: HORSE STUDY**
*Pen drawing, colored, 10.2 x 12.3 cm.*
*Basel, Kupferstichkabinett, Kunstmuseum*

# THE PLATES

I

II

Iudge More Sr Tho: Mores Father.

III

IV

V

VI

VII

Tho: Wiatt Knight.

VIII

Harry Guldeford Knight.

Sᵣ Iohn Godsalue

X

Phillip Hobbie Knight

XI

XII

S G Carow Knight

XIII

John Poines.

XIV

XV

XVI

Iohn More Sᵗ Thomas Mores Son.

XVII

XVIII

Thomas Earl of Surry

XIX

S. George of Cornwall

XX

XXI

XXII

XXIII

The Lady Eliot.

XXIV

The Lady Borow.

XXV

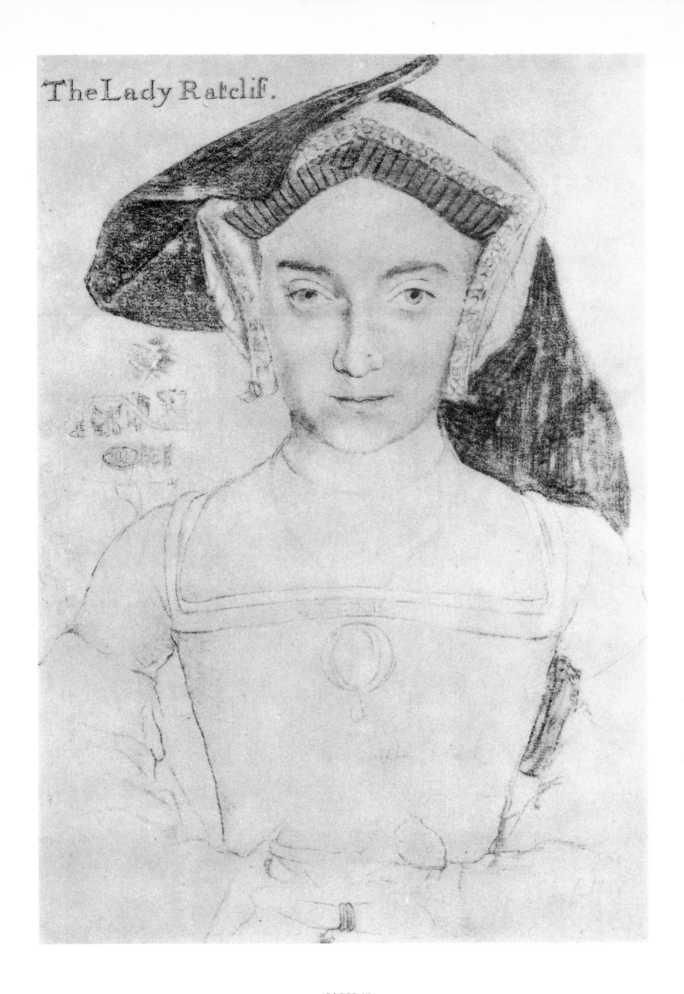

The Lady Ratclif.

XXVI

The Dutchess of Suffolk.

XXVII

XXVIII

XXIX

XXX

XXXI

XXXII

XXXIII

_Ormond_

XXXIV

XXXV

XXXVI

XXXVII

XXXVIII

XXXIX

XL

XLI

XLII

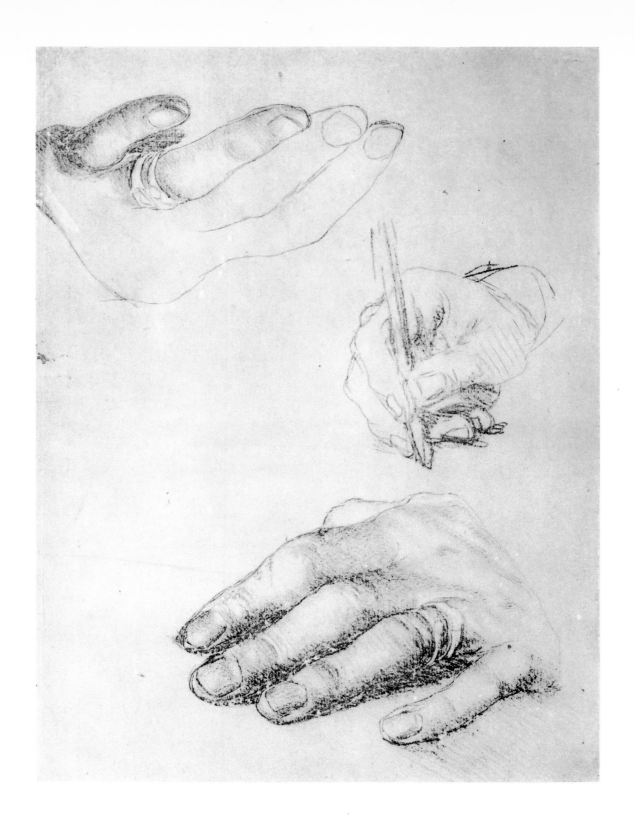

XLIII

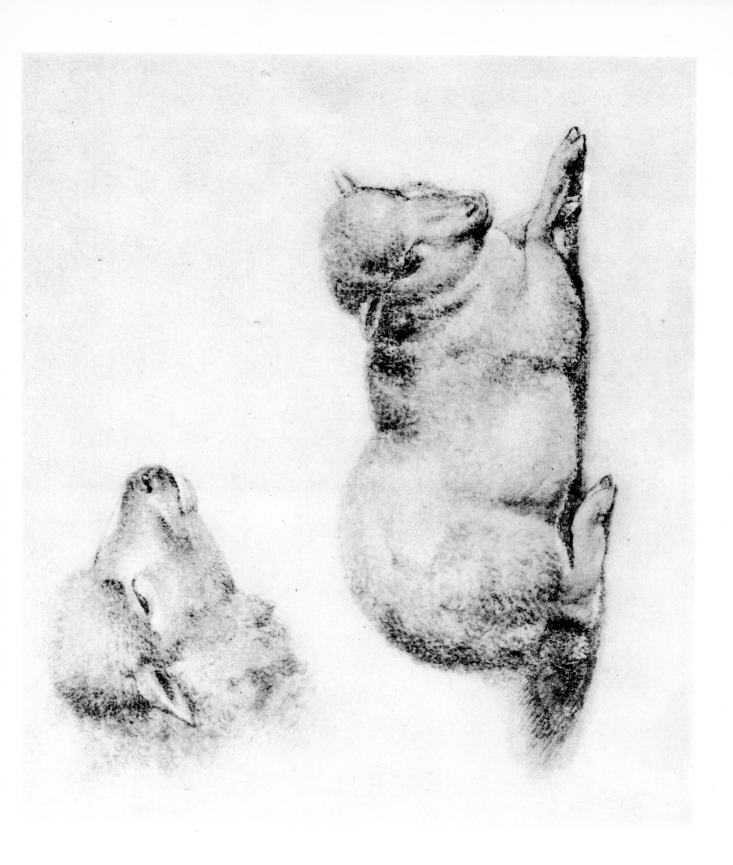

XLIV

XLV

XLVI

XLVII

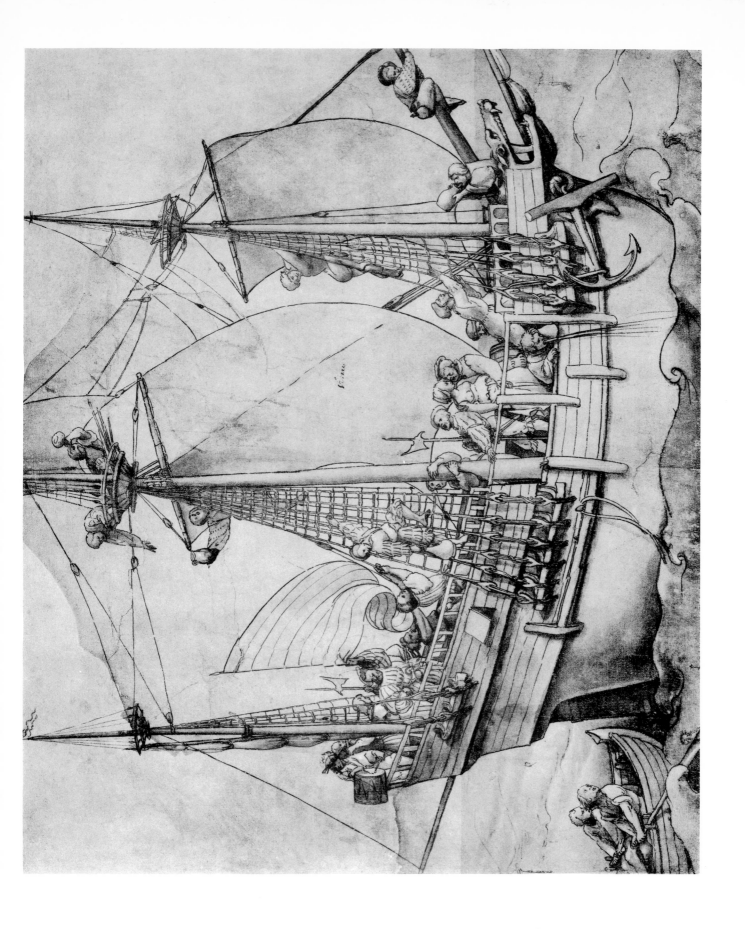

XLVIII

XLIX

LI

LII

LIII

LIV

LV

LVI

LVII